The
ABOLITION
OF
MAN

BOOKS BY C. S. LEWIS

A Grief Observed
George MacDonald: An Anthology
Mere Christianity
Miracles
The Abolition of Man
The Great Divorce
The Problem of Pain
The Screwtape Letters (with *"Screwtape Proposes a Toast"*)
The Weight of Glory

ALSO AVAILABLE FROM HARPERCOLLINS

The Chronicles of Narnia:
The Magician's Nephew
The Lion, the Witch and the Wardrobe
The Horse and His Boy
Prince Caspian
The Voyage of the Dawn Treader
The Silver Chair
The Last Battle

The
ABOLITION
OF
MAN

or
Reflections on education with special
reference to the teaching of English in
the upper forms of schools

C. S. Lewis

HarperOne
An Imprint of HarperCollinsPublishers

HarperOne

FIRST HARPERCOLLINS PAPERBACK EDITION PUBLISHED IN 2001

Library of Congress Cataloging-in-Publication Data
Lewis, C. S. (Clive Staples), 1898–1963.
The abolition of man, or, reflections on education with special
reference to the teaching of English in the upper forms of schools/
C. S. Lewis
p. cm.
Includes bibliographical references.
ISBN 978–0–06–065294–4
1. Education—Philosophy. 2. English language—Study and teaching
(Secondary). I. Title : Abolition of man. II. Title : Reflections on
education with special reference to the teaching of English in the
upper forms of schools. III. Title.
LB41.L665   2000
370'.I—dc21   00–049858

21 22 23 LSC (C) 80 79 78 77 76 75 74 73 72 71

The Master said, He who sets to work on a
different strand destroys the whole fabric
CONFUCIUS, Analects II. 16

CONTENTS

The
ABOLITION
OF
MAN

MEN WITHOUT CHESTS

So he sent the word to slay
And slew the little childer.
TRADITIONAL CAROL

I doubt whether we are sufficiently attentive to the importance of elementary text books. That is why I have chosen as the starting-point for these lectures a little book on English intended for 'boys and girls in the upper forms of schools'. I do not think the authors of this book (there were two of them) intended any harm, and I owe them, or their publisher, good language for sending me a complimentary copy. At the same time I shall have nothing good to say of them. Here is a pretty predicament. I do not want to pillory two modest practising schoolmasters who were doing the best they knew: but I cannot be silent about what I think the actual tendency of their work. I therefore propose to conceal their names. I shall refer to these gentlemen as Gaius and Titius and to their book as *The Green Book*. But I promise you there is such a book and I have it on my shelves.

In their second chapter Gaius and Titius quote the well-known story of Coleridge at the waterfall. You remember that there were two tourists present: that one called it 'sublime' and the other 'pretty'; and that Coleridge mentally endorsed the first judgement and rejected the second with disgust. Gaius and Titius comment as follows: 'When the man said *This is sublime*, he appeared to be making a remark about the waterfall . . . Actually . . . he was not making a remark about the waterfall, but a remark about his own feelings. What he was saying was really *I have feelings associated in my mind with the word "Sublime"*, or shortly, *I have sublime feelings*.' Here are a good many deep questions settled in a pretty summary fashion. But the authors are not yet finished. They add: 'This confusion is continually present in language as we use it. We appear to be saying something very important about something: and actually we are only saying something about our own feelings.'[1]

Before considering the issues really raised by this momentous little paragraph (designed, you will remember, for 'the upper forms of schools') we must eliminate one mere confusion into which Gaius and Titius have fallen. Even on their own view—on any conceivable view—the man who says *This is sublime* cannot mean *I have sublime feelings*. Even if it were granted that such qualities as sublimity were simply and solely projected into things from our own emotions, yet the emotions which prompt the projection are the correlatives, and therefore almost the opposites, of the qualities projected. The feelings which make a man call an object sublime are not sublime feelings but feelings of veneration. If *This is sublime* is to be reduced at all to a statement about the speaker's feelings, the proper translation would be *I have humble feelings*. If the view held by Gaius and Titius were consistently applied it would lead to obvious absurdities. It would force them to maintain that *You are contemptible* means *I have contemptible feelings*: in fact that *Your feelings are contemptible* means *My feelings are contemptible*. But we need not delay over this which is the very *pons asinorum* of our subject. It would be unjust to Gaius and Titius themselves to emphasize what was doubtless a mere inadvertence.

The schoolboy who reads this passage in *The Green Book* will believe two propositions: firstly, that all sentences containing a predicate of value are statements about the emotional state of the speaker, and secondly, that all such statements are unimportant. It is true that Gaius and Titius have said neither of these things in so many words. They have treated only one particular predicate of value (*sublime*) as a word descriptive of the speaker's emotions. The pupils are left to do for themselves the work of extending the same treatment to all predicates of value: and no slightest obstacle to such extension is placed in their way. The authors may or may not desire the extension: they may never have given the question five minutes' serious thought in their lives. I am not concerned with what they desired but with the effect their book will certainly have on the schoolboy's mind. In the same way, they have not said that judgements of value are unimportant. Their words are that we '*appear* to be saying something very important' when in reality we are '*only* saying something about our own feelings'. No schoolboy will be able to resist the suggestion brought to bear upon him by that word *only*. I do not mean, of course, that he will make any conscious inference from what he reads to a general philosophical theory that all values are subjective and trivial. The very power of Gaius and Titius depends on the fact that they are dealing with a boy: a boy who thinks he is 'doing' his 'English prep' and has no notion that ethics, theology, and politics are all at stake. It is not a theory they put into his mind, but an assumption, which ten years hence, its origin forgotten and its presence unconscious, will condition him to take one side in a controversy which he has never recognized as a controversy at all. The authors themselves, I suspect, hardly know what they are doing to the boy, and he cannot know what is being done to him.

Before considering the philosophical credentials of the position which Gaius and Titius have adopted about value, I should like to show its practical results on the educational procedure. In their fourth chapter they quote a silly advertisement of a pleasure cruise and proceed to inoculate their pupils against the sort of writing it exhibits.[2] The advertisement tells us that those who buy tickets for this cruise will go 'across the Western Ocean where Drake of Devon sailed', 'adventuring after the treasures of the Indies', and bringing home themselves also a 'treasure' of 'golden hours' and 'glowing colours'. It is a bad bit of writing, of course: a venal and bathetic exploitation of those emotions of awe and pleasure which men feel in visiting places that have striking associations with history or legend. If Gaius and Titius were to stick to their last and teach their readers (as they promised to do) the art of English composition, it was their business to put this advertisement side by side with passages from great writers in which the very emotion is well expressed, and then show where the difference lies.

They might have used Johnson's famous passage from the *Western Islands*, which concludes: 'That man is little to be envied, whose patriotism would not gain force upon the plain of Marathon, or whose piety would not grow warmer among the ruins of Iona.'[3] They might have taken that place in *The Prelude* where Wordsworth describes how the antiquity of London first descended on his mind with 'Weight and power, Power growing under weight'.[4] A lesson which had laid such literature beside the advertisement and really discriminated the good from the bad would have been a lesson worth teaching. There would have been some blood and sap in it—the trees of knowledge and of life growing together. It would also have had the merit of being a lesson in literature: a subject of which Gaius and Titius, despite their professed purpose, are uncommonly shy.

What they actually do is to point out that the luxurious motor-vessel won't really sail where Drake did, that the tourists will not have any adventures, that the treasures they bring home will be of a purely metaphorical nature, and that a trip to Margate might provide 'all the pleasure and rest' they required.⁵ All this is very true: talents inferior to those of Gaius and Titius would have sufficed to discover it. What they have not noticed, or not cared about, is that a very similar treatment could be applied to much good literature which treats the same emotion. What, after all, can the history of early British Christianity, in pure reason, add to the motives for piety as they exist in the eighteenth century? Why should Mr Wordsworth's inn be more comfortable or the air of London more healthy because London has existed for a long time? Or, if there is indeed any obstacle which will prevent a critic from 'debunking' Johnson and Wordsworth (and Lamb, and Virgil, and Thomas Browne, and Mr de la Mare) as *The Green Book* debunks the advertisement, Gaius and Titius have given their schoolboy readers no faintest help to its discovery.

From this passage the schoolboy will learn about literature precisely nothing. What he will learn quickly enough, and perhaps indelibly, is the belief that all emotions aroused by local association are in themselves contrary to reason and contemptible. He will have no notion that there are two ways of being immune to such an advertisement—that it falls equally flat on those who are above it and those who are below it, on the man of real sensibility and on the mere trousered ape who has never been able to conceive the Atlantic as anything more than so many million tons of cold salt water. There are two men to whom we offer in vain a false leading article on patriotism and honour: one is the coward, the other is the honourable and patriotic man. None of this is brought before the schoolboy's mind. On the contrary, he is encouraged to reject the lure of the 'Western Ocean' on the very dangerous ground that in so doing he will prove himself a knowing fellow who can't be bubbled out of his cash. Gaius and Titius, while teaching him nothing about letters, have cut out of his soul, long before he is old enough to choose, the possibility of having certain experiences which thinkers of more authority than they have held to be generous, fruitful, and humane.

But it is not only Gaius and Titius. In another little book, whose author I will call Orbilius, I find that the same operation, under the same general anaesthetic, is being carried out. Orbilius chooses for 'debunking' a silly bit of writing on horses, where these animals are praised as the 'willing servants' of the early colonists in Australia.[6] And he falls into the same trap as Gaius and Titius. Of Ruksh and Sleipnir and the weeping horses of Achilles and the warhorse in the Book of Job—nay even of Brer Rabbit and of Peter Rabbit—of man's prehistoric piety to 'our brother the ox'—of all that this semi-anthropomorphic treatment of beasts has meant in human history and of the literature where it finds noble or piquant expression—he has not a word to say.[7] Even of the problems of animal psychology as they exist for science he says nothing. He contents himself with explaining that horses are not, *secundum litteram*, interested in colonial expansion.[8] This piece of information is really all that his pupils get from him. Why the composition before them is bad, when others that lie open to the same charge are good, they do not hear. Much less do they learn of the two classes of men who are, respectively, above and below the danger of such writing—the man who really knows horses and really loves them, not with anthropomorphic illusions, but with ordinate love, and the irredeemable urban blockhead to whom a horse is merely an old-fashioned means of transport. Some pleasure in their own ponies and dogs they will have lost; some incentive to cruelty or neglect they will have received; some pleasure in their own know-ingness will have entered their minds. That is their day's lesson in English, though of English they have learned nothing. Another little portion of the human heritage has been quietly taken from them before they were old enough to understand.

I have hitherto been assuming that such teachers as Gaius and Titius do not fully realize what they are doing and do not intend the far-reaching conse-quences it will actually have. There is, of course, another possibility. What I have called (presuming on their concurrence in a certain traditional system of values) the 'trousered ape' and the 'urban blockhead' may be precisely the kind of man they really wish to produce. The differences between us may go all the way down. They may really hold that the ordinary human feelings about the past or animals or large waterfalls are contrary to reason and contemptible and ought to be eradicated. They may be intending to make a clean sweep of traditional values and start with a new set. That position will be discussed later. If it is the position which Gaius and Titius are holding, I must, for the moment, content myself with pointing out that it is a philosophical and not a literary position. In filling their book with it they have been unjust to the parent or headmaster who buys it and who has got the work of amateur philosophers where he expected the work of professional grammarians. A man would be annoyed if his son returned from the dentist with his teeth untouched and his head crammed with the dentist's *obiter dicta* on bimetallism or the Baconian theory.

But I doubt whether Gaius and Titius have really planned, under cover of teaching English, to propagate their philosophy. I think they have slipped into it for the following reasons. In the first place, literary criticism is difficult, and what they actually do is very much easier. To explain why a bad treatment of some basic human emotion is bad literature is, if we exclude all question-begging attacks on the emotion itself, a very hard thing to do. Even Dr Richards, who first seriously tackled the problem of badness in literature, failed, I think, to do it. To 'debunk' the emotion, on the basis of a commonplace rationalism, is within almost anyone's capacity. In the second place, I think Gaius and Titius may have honestly misunderstood the pressing educational need of the moment. They see the world around them swayed by emotional propaganda—they have learned from tradition that youth is sentimental—and they conclude that the best thing they can do is to fortify the minds of young people against emotion. My own experience as a teacher tells an opposite tale. For every one pupil who needs to be guarded from a weak excess of sensibility there are three who need to be awakened from the slumber of cold vulgarity. The task of the modern educator is not to cut down jungles but to irrigate deserts. The right defence against false sentiments is to inculcate just sentiments. By starving the sensibility of our pupils we only make them easier prey to the propagandist when he comes. For famished nature will be avenged and a hard heart is no infallible protection against a soft head.

But there is a third, and a profounder, reason for the procedure which Gaius and Titius adopt. They may be perfectly ready to admit that a good education should build some sentiments while destroying others. They may endeavour to do so. But it is impossible that they should succeed. Do what they will, it is the 'debunking' side of their work, and this side alone, which will really tell. In order to grasp this necessity clearly I must digress for a moment to show that what may be called the educational predicament of Gaius and Titius is different from that of all their predecessors.

Until quite modern times all teachers and even all men believed the universe to be such that certain emotional reactions on our part could be either congruous or incongruous to it—believed, in fact, that objects did not merely receive, but could *merit*, our approval or disapproval, our reverence or our contempt. The reason why Coleridge agreed with the tourist who called the cataract sublime and disagreed with the one who called it pretty was of course that he believed inanimate nature to be such that certain responses could be more 'just' or 'ordinate' or 'appropriate' to it than others. And he believed (correctly) that the tourists thought the same. The man who called the cataract sublime was not intending simply to describe his own emotions about it: he was also claiming that the object was one which *merited* those emotions. But for this claim there would be nothing to agree or disagree about. To disagree with *This is pretty* if those words simply described the lady's feelings, would be absurd: if she had said *I feel sick* Coleridge would hardly have replied *No; I feel quite well*. When Shelley, having compared the human sensibility to an Aeolian lyre, goes on to add that it differs from a lyre in having a power of 'internal adjustment' whereby it can 'accommodate its chords to the motions of that which strikes them',[9] he is assuming the same belief. 'Can you be righteous', asks Traherne, 'unless you be just in rendering to things their due esteem? All things were made to be yours and you were made to prize them according to their value.'[10]

St Augustine defines virtue as *ordo amoris*, the ordinate condition of the affections in which every object is accorded that kind of degree of love which is appropriate to it.[11] Aristotle says that the aim of education is to make the pupil like and dislike what he ought.[12] When the age for reflective thought comes, the pupil who has been thus trained in 'ordinate affections' or 'just sentiments' will easily find the first principles in Ethics; but to the corrupt man they will never be visible at all and he can make no progress in that science.[13] Plato before him had said the same. The little human animal will not at first have the right responses. It must be trained to feel pleasure, liking, disgust, and hatred at those things which really are pleasant, likeable, disgusting and hateful.[14] In the *Republic*, the well-nurtured youth is one 'who would see most clearly whatever was

amiss in ill-made works of man or ill-grown works
of nature, and with a just distaste would blame and
hate the ugly even from his earliest years and would
give delighted praise to beauty, receiving it into his
soul and being nourished by it, so that he becomes a
man of gentle heart. All this before he is of an age to
reason; so that when Reason at length comes to him,
then, bred as he has been, he will hold out his hands
in welcome and recognize her because of the affinity
he bears to her.'[15] In early Hinduism that conduct in
men which can be called good consists in confor-
mity to, or almost participation in, the *Rta*—that
great ritual or pattern of nature and supernature
which is revealed alike in the cosmic order, the
moral virtues, and the ceremonial of the temple.
Righteousness, correctness, order, the *Rta*, is con-
stantly identified with *satya* or truth, correspondence to reality. As Plato said that the Good was
'beyond existence' and Wordsworth that through
virtue the stars were strong, so the Indian masters
say that the gods themselves are born of the *Rta* and
obey it.[16]

The Chinese also speak of a great thing (the greatest thing) called the *Tao*. It is the reality beyond all predicates, the abyss that was before the Creator Himself. It is Nature, it is the Way, the Road. It is the Way in which the universe goes on, the Way in which things everlastingly emerge, stilly and tranquilly, into space and time. It is also the Way which every man should tread in imitation of that cosmic and supercosmic progression, conforming all activities to that great exemplar.[17] 'In ritual', say the *Analects*, 'it is harmony with Nature that is prized.'[18] The ancient Jews likewise praise the Law as being 'true'.[19]

This conception in all its forms, Platonic, Aristotelian, Stoic, Christian, and Oriental alike, I shall henceforth refer to for brevity simply as 'the *Tao*'. Some of the accounts of it which I have quoted will seem, perhaps, to many of you merely quaint or even magical. But what is common to them all is something we cannot neglect. It is the doctrine of objective value, the belief that certain attitudes are really true, and others really false, to the kind of thing the universe is and the kind of things we are. Those who know the *Tao* can hold that to call children delightful or old men venerable is not simply to record a psychological fact about our own parental or filial emotions at the moment, but to recognize a quality which *demands* a certain response from us whether we make it or not. I myself do not enjoy the society of small children: because I speak from within the *Tao* I recognize this as a defect in myself—just as a man may have to recognize that he is tone deaf or colour blind. And because our approvals and disapprovals are thus recognitions of objective value or responses to an objective order, therefore emotional states can be in harmony with reason (when we feel liking for what ought to be approved) or out of harmony with reason (when we perceive that liking is due but cannot feel it). No emotion is, in itself, a judgement; in that sense all emotions and sentiments are alogical. But they can be reasonable or unreasonable as they conform to Reason or fail to conform. The heart never takes the place of the head: but it can, and should, obey it.

Over against this stands the world of *The Green Book*. In it the very possibility of a sentiment being reasonable—or even unreasonable—has been excluded from the outset. It can be reasonable or unreasonable only if it conforms or fails to conform to something else. To say that the cataract is sublime means saying that our emotion of humility is appropriate or ordinate to the reality, and thus to speak of something else besides the emotion; just as to say that a shoe fits is to speak not only of shoes but of feet. But this reference to something beyond the emotion is what Gaius and Titius exclude from every sentence containing a predicate of value. Such statements, for them, refer solely to the emotion. Now the emotion, thus considered by itself, cannot be either in agreement or disagreement with Reason. It is irrational not as a paralogism is irrational, but as a physical event is irrational: it does not rise even to the dignity of error. On this view, the world of facts, without one trace of value, and the world of feelings, without one trace of truth or falsehood, justice or injustice, confront one another, and no *rapprochement* is possible.

Hence the educational problem is wholly different

according as you stand within or without the *Tao*.
For those within, the task is to train in the pupil
those responses which are in themselves appropriate,
whether anyone is making them or not, and in making which the very nature of man consists. Those
without, if they are logical, must regard all sentiments as equally non-rational, as mere mists between
us and the real objects. As a result, they must either
decide to remove all sentiments, as far as possible,
from the pupil's mind; or else to encourage some
sentiments for reasons that have nothing to do with
their intrinsic 'justness' or 'ordinacy'. The latter
course involves them in the questionable process of
creating in others by 'suggestion' or incantation a
mirage which their own reason has successfully dis-
sipated.

Perhaps this will become clearer if we take a concrete instance. When a Roman father told his son
that it was a sweet and seemly thing to die for his
country, he believed what he said. He was communi-
cating to the son an emotion which he himself shared
and which he believed to be in accord with the value

which his judgement discerned in noble death. He was giving the boy the best he had, giving of his spirit to humanize him as he had given of his body to beget him. But Gaius and Titius cannot believe that in calling such a death sweet and seemly they would be saying 'something important about something'. Their own method of debunking would cry out against them if they attempted to do so. For death is not something to eat and therefore cannot be *dulce* in the literal sense, and it is unlikely that the real sensations preceding it will be *dulce* even by analogy. And as for *decorum*—that is only a word describing how some other people will feel about your death when they happen to think of it, which won't be often, and will certainly do you no good. There are only two courses open to Gaius and Titius. Either they must go the whole way and debunk this sentiment like any other, or must set themselves to work to produce, from outside, a sentiment which they believe to be of no value to the pupil and which may cost him his life, because it is useful to us (the survivors) that our young men should feel it. If they embark on this course the difference between the old and the new education will be an important one. Where the old initiated, the new merely 'conditions'. The old dealt with its pupils as grown birds deal with young birds when they teach them to fly; the new deals with them more as the poultry-keeper deals with young birds— making them thus or thus for purposes of which the birds know nothing. In a word, the old was a kind of propagation—men transmitting manhood to men; the new is merely propaganda.

It is to their credit that Gaius and Titius embrace the first alternative. Propaganda is their abomination: not because their own philosophy gives a ground for condemning it (or anything else) but because they are better than their principles. They probably have some vague notion (I will examine it in my next lecture) that valour and good faith and justice could be sufficiently commended to the pupil on what they would call 'rational' or 'biological' or 'modern' grounds, if it should ever become necessary. In the meantime, they leave the matter alone and get on with the business of debunking.

But this course, though less inhuman, is not less disastrous than the opposite alternative of cynical propaganda. Let us suppose for a moment that the harder virtues could really be theoretically justifed with no appeal to objective value. It still remains true that no justification of virtue will enable a man to be virtuous. Without the aid of trained emotions the intellect is powerless against the animal organism. I had sooner play cards against a man who was quite sceptical about ethics, but bred to believe that 'a gentleman does not cheat', than against an irreproachable moral philosopher who had been brought up among sharpers. In battle it is not syllogisms that will keep the reluctant nerves and muscles to their post in the third hour of the bombardment. The crudest sentimentalism (such as Gaius and Titius would wince at) about a flag or a country or a regiment will be of more use. We were told it all long ago by Plato. As the king governs by his executive, so Reason in man must rule the mere appetites by means of the 'spirited element'.[20] The head rules the belly through the chest—the seat, as Alanus tells us, of Magnanimity,[21] of emotions organized by trained habit into stable sentiments. The Chest-Magnanimity-Sentiment—these are the indispensable liaison officers between cerebral man and visceral man. It may even be said that it is by this middle element that man is man: for by his intellect he is mere spirit and by his appetite mere animal.

The operation of *The Green Book* and its kind is to produce what may be called Men without Chests. It is an outrage that they should be commonly spoken of as Intellectuals. This gives them the chance to say that he who attacks them attacks Intelligence. It is not so. They are not distinguished from other men by any unusual skill in finding truth nor any virginal ardour to pursue her. Indeed it would be strange if they were: a persevering devotion to truth, a nice sense of intellectual honour, cannot be long maintained without the aid of a sentiment which Gaius and Titius could debunk as easily as any other. It is not excess of thought but defect of fertile and generous emotion that marks them out. Their heads are no bigger than the ordinary: it is the atrophy of the chest beneath that makes them seem so.

And all the time—such is the tragi-comedy of our situation—we continue to clamour for those very qualities we are rendering impossible. You can hardly open a periodical without coming across the statement that what our civilization needs is more 'drive', or dynamism, or self-sacrifice, or 'creativity'. In a sort of ghastly simplicity we remove the organ and demand the function. We make men without chests and expect of them virtue and enterprise. We laugh at honour and are shocked to find traitors in our midst. We castrate and bid the geldings be fruitful.

2

THE WAY

It is upon the Trunk that a gentleman works.
Analects OF CONFUCIUS, I.2

The practical result of education in the spirit of *The Green Book* must be the destruction of the society which accepts it. But this is not necessarily a refutation of subjectivism about values as a theory. The true doctrine might be a doctrine which if we accept we die. No one who speaks from within the *Tao* could reject it on that account: ἐν δὲ φάει καὶ ὀλεσσον. But it has not yet come to that. There are theoretical difficulties in the philosophy of Gaius and Titius.

However subjective they may be about some traditional values, Gaius and Titius have shown by the very act of writing *The Green Book* that there must be some other values about which they are not subjective at all. They write in order to produce certain states of mind in the rising generation, if not because they think those states of mind intrinsically just or good, yet certainly because they think them to be the means to some state of society which they regard as desirable. It would not be difficult to collect from various passages in *The Green Book* what their ideal is. But we need not. The important point is not the precise nature of their end, but the fact that they have an end at all. They must have, or their book (being purely practical in intention) is written to no purpose. And this end must have real value in their eyes. To abstain from calling it good and to use, instead, such predicates as 'necessary' or 'progressive' or 'efficient' would be a subterfuge. They could be forced by argument to answer the questions 'necessary for what?', 'progressing towards what?', 'effecting what?'; in the last resort they would have to admit that some state of affairs was in their opinion good for its own sake. And this time they could not maintain that 'good' simply described their own emotion about it. For the whole purpose of their book is so to condition the young reader that he will share their approval, and this would be either a fool's or a villain's undertaking unless they held that their approval was in some way valid or correct.

In actual fact Gaius and Titius will be found to hold, with complete uncritical dogmatism, the whole system of values which happened to be in vogue among moderately educated young men of the professional classes during the period between the two wars.[1] Their scepticism about values is on the surface: it is for use on other people's values; about the values current in their own set they are not nearly sceptical enough. And this phenomenon is very usual. A great many of those who 'debunk' traditional or (as they would say) 'sentimental' values have in the background values of their own which they believe to be immune from the debunking process. They claim to be cutting away the parasitic growth of emotion, religious sanction, and inherited taboos, in order that 'real' or 'basic' values may emerge. I will now try to find out what happens if this is seriously attempted.

Let us continue to use the previous example—that of death for a good cause—not, of course, because virtue is the only value or martyrdom the only virtue, but because this is the *experimentum crucis* which shows different systems of thought in the clearest light. Let us suppose that an Innovator in values regards *dulce et decorum* and *greater love hath no man* as mere irrational sentiments which are to be stripped off in order that we may get down to the 'realistic' or 'basic' ground of this value. Where will he find such a ground?

First of all, he might say that the real value lay in the utility of such sacrifice to the community. 'Good', he might say, '*means* what is useful to the community.' But of course the death of the community is not useful to the community—only the death of some of its members. What is really meant is that the death of some men is useful to other men. That is very true. But on what ground are some men being asked to die for the benefit of others? Every appeal to pride, honour, shame, or love is excluded by hypothesis. To use these would be to return to sentiment and the Innovator's task is, having cut all that away, to explain to men, in terms of pure reasoning, why they will be well advised to die that others may live. He may say 'Unless some of us *risk* death all of us are *certain* to die.' But that will be true only in a limited number of cases; and even when it is true it provokes the very reasonable counter question 'Why should I be one of those who take the risk?'

At this point the Innovator may ask why, after all, selfishness should be more 'rational' or 'intelligent' than altruism. The question is welcome. If by Reason we mean the process actually employed by Gaius and Titius when engaged in debunking (that is, the connecting by inference of propositions, ultimately derived from sense data, with further propositions), then the answer must be that a refusal to sacrifice oneself is no more rational than a consent to do so. And no less rational. Neither choice is rational—or irrational—at all. From propositions about fact alone no *practical* conclusion can ever be drawn. *This will preserve society* cannot lead to *do this* except by the mediation of *society ought to be preserved. This will cost you your life* cannot lead directly to *do not do this*: it can lead to it only through a felt desire or an acknowledged duty of self-preservation. The Innovator is trying to get a conclusion in the imperative mood out of premises in the indicative mood: and though he continues trying to all eternity he cannot succeed, for the thing is impossible. We must therefore either extend the word Reason to include what our ancestors called Practical Reason and confess that judgements such as *society ought to be preserved* (though they can support themselves by no reason of the sort that Gaius and Titius demand) are not mere sentiments but are rationality itself; or else we must give up at once, and for ever, the attempt to find a core of 'rational' value behind all the sentiments we have debunked. The Innovator will not take the first alternative, for practical principles known to all men by Reason are simply the *Tao* which he has set out to supersede. He is more likely to give up the quest for a 'rational' core and to hunt for some other ground even more 'basic' and 'realistic'.

This he will probably feel that he has found in Instinct. The preservation of society, and of the species itself, are ends that do not hang on the precarious thread of Reason: they are given by Instinct. That is why there is no need to argue against the man who does not acknowledge them. We have an instinctive urge to preserve our own species. That is why men ought to work for posterity. We have no instinctive urge to keep promises or to respect individual life: that is why scruples of justice and humanity—in fact the *Tao*—can be properly swept away when they conflict with our real end, the preservation of the species. That, again, is why the modern situation permits and demands a new sexual morality: the old taboos served some real purpose in helping to preserve the species, but contraceptives have modified this and we can now abandon many of the taboos. For of course sexual desire, being instinctive, is to be gratified whenever it does not conflict with the preservation of the species. It looks, in fact, as if an ethics based on instinct will give the Innovator all he wants and nothing that he does not want.

In reality we have not advanced one step. I will not insist on the point that Instinct is a name for we know not what (to say that migratory birds find their way by instinct is only to say that we do not know how migratory birds find their way), for I think it is here being used in a fairly definite sense, to mean an unreflective or spontaneous impulse widely felt by the members of a given species. In what way does Instinct, thus conceived, help us to find 'real' values? Is it maintained that we *must* obey Instinct, that we cannot do otherwise? But if so, why are *Green Books* and the like written? Why this stream of exhortation to drive us where we cannot help going? Why such praise for those who have submitted to the inevitable? Or is it maintained that if we do obey Instinct we shall be happy and satisfied? But the very question we are considering was that of facing death which (so far as the Innovator knows) cuts off every possible satisfaction: and if we have an instinctive desire for the good of posterity then this desire, by the very nature of the case, can never be satisfied, since its aim is achieved, if at all, when we are dead. It looks very much as if the Innovator would have to say not that we must obey Instinct, nor that it will satisfy us to do so, but that we *ought* to obey it.[2]

But why ought we to obey Instinct? Is there another instinct of a higher order directing us to do so, and a third of a still higher order directing us to obey *it*?—an infinite regress of instincts? This is presumably impossible, but nothing else will serve. From the statement about psychological fact 'I have an impulse to do so and so' we cannot by any ingenuity derive the practical principle 'I ought to obey this impulse'. Even if it were true that men had a spontaneous, unreflective impulse to sacrifice their own lives for the preservation of their fellows, it remains a quite separate question whether this is an impulse they should control or one they should indulge. For even the Innovator admits that many impulses (those which conflict with the preservation of the species) have to be controlled. And this admission surely introduces us to a yet more fundamental difficulty.

Telling us to obey Instinct is like telling us to obey 'people'. People say different things: so do instincts.

Our instincts are at war. If it is held that the instinct for preserving the species should always be obeyed at the expense of other instincts, whence do we derive this rule of precedence? To listen to that instinct speaking in its own cause and deciding it in its own favour would be rather simple-minded. Each instinct, if you listen to it, will claim to be gratified at the expense of all the rest. By the very act of listening to one rather than to others we have already pre-judged the case. If we did not bring to the examination of our instincts a knowledge of their comparative dignity we could never learn it from them. And that knowledge cannot itself be instinctive: the judge cannot be one of the parties judged; or, if he is, the decision is worthless and there is no ground for placing the preservation of the species above self-preservation or sexual appetite.

The idea that, without appealing to any court higher than the instincts themselves, we can yet find grounds for preferring one instinct above its fellows dies very hard. We grasp at useless words: we call it the 'basic', or 'fundamental', or 'primal', or 'deepest' instinct. It is of no avail. Either these words conceal a value judgement passed *upon* the instinct and therefore not derivable *from* it, or else they merely record its felt intensity, the frequency of its operation and its wide distribution. If the former, the whole attempt to base value upon instinct has been abandoned: if the latter, these observations about the quantitative aspects of a psychological event lead to no practical conclusion. It is the old dilemma. Either the premisses already concealed an imperative or the conclusion remains merely in the indicative.[3]

Finally, it is worth inquiry whether there *is* any instinct to care for posterity or preserve the species. I do not discover it in myself: and yet I am a man rather prone to think of remote futurity—a man who can read Mr Olaf Stapledon with delight. Much less do I find it easy to believe that the majority of people who have sat opposite me in buses or stood with me in queues feel an unreflective impulse to do anything at all about the species, or posterity. Only people educated in a particular way have ever had the idea 'posterity' before their minds at all. It is difficult to assign to instinct our attitude towards an object which exists only for reflective men. What we have by nature is an impulse to preserve our own children and grandchildren; an impulse which grows progressively feebler as the imagination looks forward and finally dies out in the 'deserts of vast futurity'. No parents who were guided by this instinct would dream for a moment of setting up the claims of their hypothetical descendants against those of the baby actually crowing and kicking in the room. Those of us who accept the *Tao* may, perhaps, say that they ought to do so: but that is not open to those who treat instinct as the source of value. As we pass from mother love to rational planning for the future we are passing away from the realm of instinct into that of choice and reflection: and if instinct is the source of value, planning for the future ought to be less respectable and less obligatory than the baby language and cuddling of the fondest mother or the most fatuous nursery anecdotes of a doting father. If we are to base ourselves upon instinct, these things are the substance, and care for posterity the shadow—the huge, flickering shadow of the nursery happiness cast upon the screen of the unknown future. I do not say this projection is a bad thing: but then I do not believe that instinct is the ground of value judgements. What is absurd is to claim that your care for posterity finds its justification in instinct and then flout at every turn the only instinct on which it could be supposed to rest, tearing the child almost from the breast to crèche and kindergarten in the interests of progress and the coming race.

The truth finally becomes apparent that neither in any operation with factual propositions nor in any appeal to instinct can the Innovator find the basis for a system of values. None of the principles he requires are to be found there: but they are all to be found somewhere else. 'All within the four seas are his brothers' (xii. 5) says Confucius of the *Chün-tzu*, the *cuor gentil* or gentleman. *Humani nihil a me alienum puto* says the Stoic. 'Do as you would be done by,' says Jesus. 'Humanity is to be preserved,' says Locke.[4] All the practical principles behind the Innovator's case for posterity, or society, or the species, are there from time immemorial in the *Tao*. But they are nowhere else. Unless you accept these without question as being to the world of action what axioms are to the world of theory, you can have no practical principles whatever. You cannot reach them as conclusions: they are premisses. You may, since they can give no 'reason' for themselves of a kind to silence Gaius and Titius, regard them as sentiments: but then you must give up contrasting 'real' or 'rational' value with sentimental value. All value will be sentimental; and you must confess (on pain of abandoning every value) that all sentiment is not 'merely' subjective. You may, on the other hand, regard them as rational—nay as rationality itself—as things so obviously reasonable that they neither demand nor admit proof. But then you must allow that Reason can be practical, that an *ought* must not be dismissed because it cannot produce some *is* as its credential. If nothing is self-evident, nothing can be proved. Similarly if nothing is obligatory for its own sake, nothing is obligatory at all.

To some it will appear that I have merely restored under another name what they always meant by basic or fundamental instinct. But much more than a choice of words is involved. The Innovator attacks traditional values (the *Tao*) in defence of what he at first supposes to be (in some special sense) 'rational' or 'biological' values. But as we have seen, all the values which he uses in attacking the *Tao*, and even claims to be substituting for it, are themselves derived from the *Tao*. If he had really started from scratch, from right outside the human tradition of value, no jugglery could have advanced him an inch towards the conception that a man should die for the community or work for posterity. If the *Tao* falls, all his own conceptions of value fall with it. Not one of them can claim any authority other than that of the *Tao*. Only by such shreds of the *Tao* as he has inherited is he enabled even to attack it. The question therefore arises what title he has to select bits of it for acceptance and to reject others. For if the bits he rejects have no authority, neither have those he retains: if what he retains is valid, what he rejects is equally valid too.

The Innovator, for example, rates high the claims of posterity. He cannot get any valid claim for posterity out of instinct or (in the modern sense) reason. He is really deriving our duty to posterity from the *Tao*; our duty to do good to all men is an axiom of Practical Reason, and our duty to do good to our descendants is a clear deduction from it. But then, in every form of the *Tao* which has come down to us, side by side with the duty to children and descendants lies the duty to parents and ancestors. By what right do we reject one and accept the other? Again, the Innovator may place economic value first. To get people fed and clothed is the great end, and in pursuit of its scruples about justice and good faith may be set aside. The *Tao* of course agrees with him about the importance of getting the people fed and clothed. Unless the Innovator were himself using the *Tao* he could never have learned of such a duty. But side by side with it in the *Tao* lie those duties of justice and good faith which he is ready to debunk. What is his warrant? He may be a Jingoist, a Racialist, an extreme nationalist, who maintains that the advancement of his own people is the object to which all else ought to yield. But no kind of factual observation and no appeal to instinct will give him a ground for this option. Once more, he is in fact deriving it from the *Tao*: a duty to our own kin, because they are our own kin, is a part of traditional morality. But side by side with it in the *Tao*, and limiting it, lie the inflexible demands of justice, and the rule that, in the long run, all men are our brothers. Whence comes the Innovator's authority to pick and choose?

Since I can see no answer to these questions, I draw the following conclusions. This thing which I have called for convenience the *Tao*, and which others may call Natural Law or Traditional Morality or the First Principles of Practical Reason or the First Platitudes, is not one among a series of possible systems of value. It is the sole source of all value judgements. If it is rejected, all value is rejected. If any value is retained, it is retained. The effort to refute it and raise a new system of value in its place is self-contradictory. There has never been, and never will be, a radically new judgement of value in the history of the world. What purport to be new systems or (as they now call them) 'ideologies', all consist of fragments from the *Tao* itself, arbitrarily wrenched from their context in the whole and then swollen to madness in their isolation, yet still owing to the *Tao* and to it alone such validity as they possess. If my duty to my parents is a superstition, then so is my duty to posterity. If justice is a superstition, then so is my duty to my country or my race. If the pursuit of scientific knowledge is a real value, then so is conjugal fidelity. The rebellion of new ideologies against the *Tao* is a rebellion of the branches against the tree: if the rebels could succeed they would find that they had destroyed themselves. The human mind has no more power of inventing a new value than of imagining a new primary colour, or, indeed, of creating a new sun and a new sky for it to move in.

Does this mean, then, that no progress in our perceptions of value can ever take place? That we are bound down for ever to an unchanging code given once for all? And is it, in any event, possible to talk of obeying what I call the *Tao*? If we lump together, as I have done, the traditional moralities of East and

West, the Christian, the Pagan, and the Jew, shall we not find many contradictions and some absurdities? I admit all this. Some criticism, some removal of contradictions, even some real development, is required. But there are two very different kinds of criticism.

A theorist about language may approach his native tongue, as it were from outside, regarding its genius as a thing that has no claim on him and advocating wholesale alterations of its idiom and spelling in the interests of commercial convenience or scientific accuracy. That is one thing. A great poet, who has 'loved, and been well nurtured in, his mother tongue', may also make great alterations in it, but his changes of the language are made in the spirit of the language itself: he works from within. The language which suffers, has also inspired the changes. That is a different thing—as different as the works of Shakespeare are from Basic English. It is the difference between alteration from within and alteration from without: between the organic and the surgical.

In the same way, the *Tao* admits development from within. There is a difference between a real moral advance and a mere innovation. From the Confucian 'Do not do to others what you would not like them to do to you' to the Christian 'Do as you would be done by' is a real advance. The morality of Nietzsche is a mere innovation. The first is an advance because no one who did not admit the validity of the old maxim could see reason for accepting the new one, and anyone who accepted the old would at once recognize the new as an extension of the same principle. If he rejected it, he would have to reject it as a superfluity, something that went too far, not as something simply heterogeneous from his own ideas of value. But the Nietzschean ethic can be accepted only if we are ready to scrap traditional morals as a mere error and then to put ourselves in a position where we can find no ground for any value judgements at all. It is the difference between a man who says to us: 'You like your vegetables moderately fresh; why not grow your own and have them perfectly fresh?' and a man who says, 'Throw away that loaf and try eating bricks and centipedes instead.'

Those who understand the spirit of the *Tao* and who have been led by that spirit can modify it in directions which that spirit itself demands. Only they can know what those directions are. The outsider knows nothing about the matter. His attempts at alteration, as we have seen, contradict themselves. So far from being able to harmonize discrepancies in its letter by penetration to its spirit, he merely snatches at some one precept, on which the accidents of time and place happen to have riveted his attention, and then rides it to death—for no reason that he can give. From within the *Tao* itself comes the only authority to modify the *Tao*. This is what Confucius meant when he said 'With those who follow a different Way it is useless to take counsel'.[5] This is why Aristotle said that only those who have been well brought up can usefully study ethics: to the corrupted man, the man who stands outside the *Tao*, the very starting point of this science is invisible.[6] He may be hostile, but he cannot be critical: he does not know what is being discussed. This is why it was also said 'This people that knoweth not the Law is accursed'[7] and 'He that believeth not shall be damned'.[8] An open mind, in questions that are not ultimate, is useful. But an open mind about the ultimate foundations either of Theoretical or of Practical Reason is idiocy. If a man's mind is open on these things, let his mouth at least be shut. He can say nothing to the purpose. Outside the *Tao* there is no ground for criticizing either the *Tao* or anything else.

In particular instances it may, no doubt, be a matter of some delicacy to decide where the legitimate internal criticism ends and the fatal external kind begins. But wherever any precept of traditional morality is simply challenged to produce its credentials, as though the burden of proof lay on it, we have taken the wrong position. The legitimate reformer endeavours to show that the precept in question conflicts with some precept which its defenders allow to be more fundamental, or that it does not really embody the judgement of value it professes to embody. The direct frontal attack 'Why?'—'What good does it do?'—'Who said so?' is never permissible; not because it is harsh or offensive but because no values at all can justify them-selves on that level. If you persist in *that* kind of trial you will destroy all values, and so destroy the bases of your own criticism as well as the thing criticized. You must not hold a pistol to the head of the *Tao*. Nor must we postpone obedience to a precept until its credentials have been examined. Only those who are practising the *Tao* will understand it. It is the well-nurtured man, the *cuor gentil*, and he alone, who can recognize Reason when it comes.[9] It is Paul, the Pharisee, the man 'perfect as touching the Law' who learns where and how that Law was deficient.[10]

In order to avoid misunderstanding, I may add that though I myself am a Theist, and indeed a Christian, I am not here attempting any indirect argument for Theism. I am simply arguing that if we are to have values at all we must accept the ultimate platitudes of Practical Reason as having absolute validity: that any attempt, having become sceptical about these, to reintroduce value lower down on some supposedly more 'realistic' basis, is doomed. Whether this position implies a supernatural origin for the *Tao* is a question I am not here concerned with.

Yet how can the modern mind be expected to embrace the conclusion we have reached? This *Tao* which, it seems, we must treat as an absolute is simply a phenomenon like any other—the reflection upon the minds of our ancestors of the agricultural rhythm in which they lived or even of their physiology. We know already in principle how such things are produced: soon we shall know in detail: eventually we shall be able to produce them at will. Of course, while we did not know how minds were made, we accepted this mental furniture as a datum, even as a master. But many things in nature which were once our masters have become our servants. Why not this? Why must our conquest of nature stop short, in stupid reverence, before this final and toughest bit of 'nature' which has hitherto been called the conscience of man? You threaten us with some obscure disaster if we step outside it: but we have been threatened in that way by obscurantists at every step in our advance, and each time the threat has proved false.

You say we shall have no values at all if we step out-side the *Tao*. Very well: we shall probably find that we can get on quite comfortably without them. Let us regard all ideas of what we *ought* to do simply as an interesting psychological survival: let us step right out of all that and start doing what we like. Let us decide for ourselves what man is to be and make him into that: not on any ground of imagined value, but because we want him to be such. Having mastered our environment, let us now master ourselves and choose our own destiny.

This is a very possible position: and those who hold it cannot be accused of self-contradiction like the half-hearted sceptics who still hope to find 'real' values when they have debunked the traditional ones. This is the rejection of the concept of value altogether. I shall need another lecture to consider it.

3

THE ABOLITION OF MAN

It came burning hot into my mind, whatever he said and however he flattered, when he got me home to his house, he would sell me for a slave.

JOHN BUNYAN

'Man's conquest of Nature' is an expression often used to describe the progress of applied science. 'Man has Nature whacked,' said someone to a friend of mine not long ago. In their context the words had a certain tragic beauty, for the speaker was dying of tuberculosis. 'No matter,' he said, 'I know I'm one of the casualties. Of course there are casualties on the winning as well as on the losing side. But that doesn't alter the fact that it is winning.' I have chosen this story as my point of departure in order to make it clear that I do not wish to disparage all that is really beneficial in the process described as 'Man's conquest', much less all the real devotion and self-sacrifice that has gone to make it possible. But having done so I must proceed to analyse this conception a little more closely. In what sense is Man the possessor of increasing power over Nature?

Let us consider three typical examples: the aeroplane, the wireless, and the contraceptive. In a civilized community, in peace-time, anyone who can pay for them may use these things. But it cannot strictly be said that when he does so he is exercising his own proper or individual power over Nature. If I pay you to carry me, I am not therefore myself a strong man. Any or all of the three things I have mentioned can be withheld from some men by other men—by those who sell, or those who allow the sale, or those who own the sources of production, or those who make the goods. What we call Man's power is, in reality, a power possessed by some men which they may, or may not, allow other men to profit by. Again, as regards the powers manifested in the aeroplane or the wireless, Man is as much the patient or subject as the possessor, since he is the target both for bombs and for propaganda. And as regards contraceptives, there is a paradoxical, negative sense in which all possible future generations are the patients or subjects of a power wielded by those already alive. By contraception simply, they are denied existence; by contraception used as a means of selective breeding, they are, without their concurring voice, made to be what one generation, for its own reasons, may choose to prefer. From this point of view, what we call Man's power over Nature turns out to be a power exercised by some men over other men with Nature as its instrument.

It is, of course, a commonplace to complain that men have hitherto used badly, and against their fellows, the powers that science has given them. But that is not the point I am trying to make. I am not speaking of particular corruptions and abuses which an increase of moral virtue would cure: I am considering what the thing called 'Man's power over Nature' must always and essentially be. No doubt, the picture could be modified by public ownership of raw materials and factories and public control of scientific research. But unless we have a world state this will still mean the power of one nation over others. And even within the world state or the nation it will mean (in principle) the power of majorities over minorities, and (in the concrete) of a government over the people. And all long-term exercises of power, especially in breeding, must mean the power of earlier generations over later ones.

The latter point is not always sufficiently emphasized, because those who write on social matters have not yet learned to imitate the physicists by always including Time among the dimensions. In order to understand fully what Man's power over Nature, and therefore the power of some men over other men, really means, we must picture the race extended in time from the date of its emergence to that of its extinction. Each generation exercises power over its successors: and each, in so far as it modifies the environment bequeathed to it and rebels against tradition, resists and limits the power of its predecessors. This modifies the picture which is sometimes painted of a progressive emancipation from tradition and a progressive control of natural processes resulting in a continual increase of human power. In reality, of course, if any one age really attains, by eugenics and scientific education, the power to make its descendants what it pleases, all men who live after it are the patients of that power. They are weaker, not stronger: for though we may have put wonderful machines in their hands we have pre-ordained how they are to use them. And if, as is almost certain, the age which had thus attained maximum power over posterity were also the age most emancipated from tradition, it would be engaged in reducing the power of its predecessors almost as drastically as that of its successors. And we must also remember that, quite apart from this, the later a generation comes—the nearer it lives to that date at which the species becomes extinct—the less power it will have in the forward direction, because its subjects will be so few. There is therefore no question of a power vested in the race as a whole steadily growing as long as the race survives. The last men, far from being the heirs of power, will be of all men most subject to the dead hand of the great planners and conditioners and will themselves exercise least power upon the future.

The real picture is that of one dominant age—let us suppose the hundredth century A.D.—which resists all previous ages most successfully and dominates all subsequent ages most irresistibly, and thus is the real master of the human species. But then within this master generation (itself an infinitesimal minority of the species) the power will be exercised by a minority smaller still. Man's conquest of Nature, if the dreams of some scientific planners are realized, means the rule of a few hundreds of men over billions upon billions of men. There neither is nor can be any simple increase of power on Man's side. Each new power won *by* man is a power *over* man as well. Each advance leaves him weaker as well as stronger. In every victory, besides being the general who triumphs, he is also the prisoner who follows the triumphal car.

I am not yet considering whether the total result of such ambivalent victories is a good thing or a bad.

I am only making clear what Man's conquest of Nature really means and especially that final stage in the conquest, which, perhaps, is not far off. The final stage is come when Man by eugenics, by pre-natal conditioning, and by an education and propaganda based on a perfect applied psychology, has obtained full control over himself. *Human* nature will be the last part of Nature to surrender to Man. The battle will then be won. We shall have 'taken the thread of life out of the hand of Clotho' and be henceforth free to make our species whatever we wish it to be. The battle will indeed be won. But who, precisely, will have won it?

For the power of Man to make himself what he pleases means, as we have seen, the power of some men to make other men what *they* please. In all ages, no doubt, nurture and instruction have, in some sense, attempted to exercise this power. But the situation to which we must look forward will be novel in two respects. In the first place, the power will be enormously increased. Hitherto the plans of educationalists have achieved very little of what they

attempted and indeed, when we read them—how
Plato would have every infant 'a bastard nursed in a
bureau', and Elyot would have the boy see no men
before the age of seven and, after that, no women,[1]
and how Locke wants children to have leaky shoes
and no turn for poetry[2]—we may well thank the
beneficent obstinacy of real mothers, real nurses, and
(above all) real children for preserving the human
race in such sanity as it still possesses. But the man-
moulders of the new age will be armed with the powers of an omnicompetent state and an irresistible
scientific technique: we shall get at last a race of conditioners who really can cut out all posterity in what
shape they please.

The second difference is even more important. In
the older systems both the kind of man the teachers
wished to produce and their motives for producing
him were prescribed by the *Tao*—a norm to which
the teachers themselves were subject and from
which they claimed no liberty to depart. They did
not cut men to some pattern they had chosen. They
handed on what they had received: they initiated the

young neophyte into the mystery of humanity which over-arched him and them alike. It was but old birds teaching young birds to fly. This will be changed. Values are now mere natural phenomena. Judgements of value are to be produced in the pupil as part of the conditioning. Whatever *Tao* there is will be the product, not the motive, of education. The conditioners have been emancipated from all that. It is one more part of Nature which they have conquered. The ultimate springs of human action are no longer, for them, something given. They have surrendered—like electricity: it is the function of the Conditioners to control, not to obey them. They know how to *produce* conscience and decide what kind of conscience they will produce. They themselves are outside, above. For we are assuming the last stage of Man's struggle with Nature. The final victory has been won. Human nature has been conquered—and, of course, has conquered, in whatever sense those words may now bear.

The Conditioners, then, are to choose what kind of artificial *Tao* they will, for their own good reasons, produce in the Human race. They are the motivators, the creators of motives. But how are they going to be motivated themselves?

For a time, perhaps, by survivals, within their own minds, of the old 'natural' *Tao*. Thus at first they may look upon themselves as servants and guardians of humanity and conceive that they have a 'duty' to do it 'good'. But it is only by confusion that they can remain in this state. They recognize the concept of duty as the result of certain processes which they can now control. Their victory has consisted precisely in emerging from the state in which they were acted upon by those processes to the state in which they use them as tools. One of the things they now have to decide is whether they will, or will not, so condition the rest of us that we can go on having the old idea of duty and the old reactions to it. How can duty help them to decide that? Duty itself is up for trial: it cannot also be the judge. And 'good' fares no better. They know quite well how to produce a dozen different conceptions of good in us. The question is which, if any, they should produce. No conception of good can help them to decide. It is absurd to fix on one of the things they are comparing and make it the standard of comparison.

To some it will appear that I am inventing a factitious difficulty for my Conditioners. Other, more simple-minded, critics may ask, 'Why should you suppose they will be such bad men?' But I am not supposing them to be bad men. They are, rather, not men (in the old sense) at all. They are, if you like, men who have sacrificed their own share in traditional humanity in order to devote themselves to the task of deciding what 'Humanity' shall henceforth mean. 'Good' and 'bad', applied to them, are words without content: for it is from them that the content of these words is henceforward to be derived. Nor is their difficulty factitious. We might suppose that it was possible to say 'After all, most of us want more or less the same things—food and drink and sexual intercourse, amusement, art, science, and the longest possible life for individuals and for the species. Let them simply say, This is what we happen to like, and go on to condition men in the way most likely to produce it.

Where's the trouble?' But this will not answer. In the first place, it is false that we all really like the same things. But even if we did, what motive is to impel the Conditioners to scorn delights and live laborious days in order that we, and posterity, may have what we like? Their duty? But that is only the *Tao*, which they may decide to impose on us, but which cannot be valid for them. If they accept it, then they are no longer the makers of conscience but still its subjects, and their final conquest over Nature has not really happened. The preservation of the species? But why should the species be preserved? One of the questions before them is whether this feeling for posterity (they know well how it is produced) shall be continued or not. However far they go back, or down, they can find no ground to stand on. Every motive they try to act on becomes at once a *petitio*. It is not that they are bad men. They are not men at all. Stepping outside the *Tao*, they have stepped into the void. Nor are their subjects necessarily unhappy men. They are not men at all: they are artefacts. Man's final conquest has proved to be the abolition of Man.

Yet the Conditioners will act. When I said just now that all motives fail them, I should have said all motives except one. All motives that claim any validity other than that of their felt emotional weight at a given moment have failed them. Everything except the *sic volo*, *sic jubeo* has been explained away. But what never claimed objectivity cannot be destroyed by subjectivism. The impulse to scratch when I itch or to pull to pieces when I am inquisitive is immune from the solvent which is fatal to my justice, or honour, or care for posterity. When all that says 'it is good' has been debunked, what says 'I want' remains. It cannot be exploded or 'seen through' because it never had any pretentions. The Conditioners, therefore, must come to be motivated simply by their own pleasure. I am not here speaking of the corrupting influence of power nor expressing the fear that under it our Conditioners will degenerate. The very words *corrupt* and *degenerate* imply a doctrine of value and are therefore meaningless in this context. My point is that those who stand outside all judgements of value cannot have any ground for preferring one of their own impulses to another except the emotional strength of that impulse.

We may legitimately hope that among the impulses which arise in minds thus emptied of all 'rational' or 'spiritual' motives, some will be benevolent. I am very doubtful myself whether the benevolent impulses, stripped of that preference and encouragement which the *Tao* teaches us to give them and left to their merely natural strength and frequency as psychological events, will have much influence. I am very doubtful whether history shows us one example of a man who, having stepped outside traditional morality and attained power, has used that power benevolently. I am inclined to think that the Conditioners will hate the conditioned. Though regarding as an illusion the artificial conscience which they produce in us their subjects, they will yet perceive that it creates in us an illusion of meaning for our lives which compares favourably with the futility of their own: and they will envy us as eunuchs envy men. But I do not insist on this, for it is a mere conjecture. What is not conjecture is that our hope even of a 'conditioned' happiness rests on what is ordinarily called 'chance'—the chance that benevolent impulses may on the whole predominate in our Conditioners. For without the judgement 'Benevolence is good'—that is, without re-entering the *Tao*—they can have no ground for promoting or stabilizing these impulses rather than any others. By the logic of their position they must just take their impulses as they come, from chance. And Chance here means Nature. It is from heredity, digestion, the weather, and the association of ideas, that the motives of the Conditioners will spring. Their extreme rationalism, by 'seeing through' all 'rational' motives, leaves them creatures of wholly irrational behaviour. If you will not obey the *Tao*, or else commit suicide, obedience to impulse (and therefore, in the long run, to mere 'nature') is the only course left open.

At the moment, then, of Man's victory over Nature, we find the whole human race subjected to some individual men, and those individuals subjected to that in themselves which is purely 'natural'—to their irrational impulses. Nature, untrammelled by values, rules the Conditioners and, through them, all humanity. Man's conquest of Nature turns out, in the moment of its consummation, to be Nature's conquest of Man. Every victory we seemed to win has led us, step by step, to this conclusion. All Nature's apparent reverses have been but tactical withdrawals. We thought we were beating her back when she was luring us on. What looked to us like hands held up in surrender was really the opening of arms to enfold us for ever. If the fully planned and conditioned world (with its *Tao* a mere product of the planning) comes into existence, Nature will be troubled no more by the restive species that rose in revolt against her so many millions of years ago, will be vexed no longer by its chatter of truth and mercy and beauty and happiness. *Ferum victorem cepit*: and if the eugenics are efficient enough there will be no second revolt, but all snug beneath the Conditioners, and the Conditioners beneath her, till the moon falls or the sun grows cold.

My point may be clearer to some if it is put in a different form. Nature is a word of varying meanings, which can best be understood if we consider its various opposites. The Natural is the opposite of the Artificial, the Civil, the Human, the Spiritual, and the Supernatural. The Artificial does not now concern us. If we take the rest of the list of opposites, however, I think we can get a rough idea of what men have meant by Nature and what it is they oppose to her. Nature seems to be the spatial and temporal, as distinct from what is less fully so or not so at all. She seems to be the world of quantity, as against the world of quality; of objects as against consciousness; of the bound, as against the wholly or partially autonomous; of that which knows no values as against that which both has and perceives value; of efficient causes (or, in some modern systems, of no causality at all) as against final causes. Now I take it that when we understand a thing analytically and then dominate and use it for our own convenience, we reduce it to the level of 'Nature' in the sense that we suspend our judgements of value about it, ignore its final cause (if any), and treat it in terms of quantity. This repression of elements in what would otherwise be our total reaction to it is sometimes very noticeable and even painful: something has to be overcome before we can cut up a dead man or a live animal in a dissecting room. These objects *resist* the movement of the mind whereby we thrust them into the world of mere Nature. But in other instances too, a similar price is exacted for our analytical knowledge and manipulative power, even if we have ceased to count it. We do not look at trees either as Dryads or as beautiful objects while we cut them into beams: the first man who did so may have felt the price keenly, and the bleeding trees in Virgil and Spenser may be far-off echoes of that primeval sense of impiety. The stars lost their divinity as astronomy developed, and the Dying God has no place in chemical agriculture. To many, no doubt, this process is simply the gradual discovery that the real world is different from what we expected, and the old opposition to Galileo or to 'body-snatchers' is simply obscurantism. But that is not the whole story. It is not the greatest of modern scientists who feel most sure that the object, stripped of its qualitative properties and reduced to mere quantity, is wholly real.

Little scientists, and little unscientific followers of science, may think so. The great minds know very well that the object, so treated, is an artificial abstraction, that something of its reality has been lost.

From this point of view the conquest of Nature appears in a new light. We reduce things to mere Nature *in order that* we may 'conquer' them. We are always conquering Nature, *because* 'Nature' is the name for what we have, to some extent, conquered. The price of conquest is to treat a thing as mere Nature. Every conquest over Nature increases her domain. The stars do not become Nature till we can weigh and measure them: the soul does not become Nature till we can psychoanalyse her. The wresting of powers *from* Nature is also the surrendering of things *to* Nature. As long as this process stops short of the final stage we may well hold that the gain outweighs the loss. But as soon as we take the final step of reducing our own species to the level of mere Nature, the whole process is stultified, for this time the being who stood to gain and the being who has been sacrificed are one and the same. This is one of the many instances where to carry a principle to what seems its logical conclusion produces absurdity. It is like the famous Irishman who found that a certain kind of stove reduced his fuel bill by half and thence concluded that two stoves of the same kind would enable him to warm his house with no fuel at all. It is the magician's bargain: give up our soul, get power in return. But once our souls, that is, ourselves, have been given up, the power thus conferred will not belong to us. We shall in fact be the slaves and puppets of that to which we have given our souls. It is in Man's power to treat himself as a mere 'natural object' and his own judgements of value as raw material for scientific manipulation to alter at will. The objection to his doing so does not lie in the fact that this point of view (like one's first day in a dissecting room) is painful and shocking till we grow used to it. The pain and the shock are at most a warning and a symptom. The real objection is that if man chooses to treat himself as raw material, raw material he will be: not raw material to be manipulated, as he fondly imagined, by himself, but by mere appetite, that is, mere Nature, in the person of his de-humanized Conditioners.

We have been trying, like Lear, to have it both ways: to lay down our human prerogative and yet at the same time to retain it. It is impossible. Either we are rational spirit obliged for ever to obey the absolute values of the *Tao*, or else we are mere nature to be kneaded and cut into new shapes for the pleasures of masters who must, by hypothesis, have no motive but their own 'natural' impulses. Only the *Tao* provides a common human law of action which can over-arch rulers and ruled alike. A dogmatic belief in objective value is necessary to the very idea of a rule which is not tyranny or an obedience which is not slavery.

I am not here thinking solely, perhaps not even chiefly, of those who are our public enemies at the moment. The process which, if not checked, will abolish Man goes on apace among Communists and Democrats no less than among Fascists. The methods may (at first) differ in brutality. But many a mild-eyed scientist in pince-nez, many a popular dramatist, many an amateur philosopher in our midst, means in the long run just the same as the Nazi rulers of Germany. Traditional values are to be 'debunked' and mankind to be cut out into some fresh shape at the will (which must, by hypothesis, be an arbitrary will) of some few lucky people in one lucky generation which has learned how to do it. The belief that we can invent 'ideologies' at pleasure, and the consequent treatment of mankind as mere ὕλη, specimens, preparations, begins to affect our very language. Once we killed bad men: now we liquidate unsocial elements. Virtue has become *integration* and diligence *dynamism*, and boys likely to be worthy of a commission are 'potential officer material'. Most wonderful of all, the virtues of thrift and temperance, and even of ordinary intelligence, are *salesresistance*.

The true significance of what is going on has been concealed by the use of the abstraction Man. Not that the word Man is necessarily a pure abstraction. In the *Tao* itself, as long as we remain within it, we find the concrete reality in which to participate is to be truly human: the real common will and common reason of humanity, alive, and growing like a tree, and branching out, as the situation varies, into ever new beauties and dignities of application. While we speak from within the *Tao* we can speak of Man having power over himself in a sense truly analogous to an individual's self-control. But the moment we step outside and regard the *Tao* as a mere subjective product, this possibility has disappeared. What is now common to all men is a mere abstract universal, an H.C.F., and Man's conquest of himself means simply the rule of the Conditioners over the conditioned human material, the world of post-humanity which, some knowingly and some unknowingly, nearly all men in all nations are at present labouring to produce.

Nothing I can say will prevent some people from describing this lecture as an attack on science. I deny the charge, of course: and real Natural Philosophers (there are some now alive) will perceive that in defending value I defend *inter alia* the value of knowledge, which must die like every other when its roots in the *Tao* are cut. But I can go further than that. I even suggest that from Science herself the cure might come.

I have described as a 'magician's bargain' that process whereby man surrenders object after object, and finally himself, to Nature in return for power. And I meant what I said. The fact that the scientist has succeeded where the magician failed has put such a wide contrast between them in popular thought that the real story of the birth of Science is misunderstood. You will even find people who write about the sixteenth century as if Magic were a medieval survival and Science the new thing that came in to sweep it away. Those who have studied the period know better. There was very little magic in the Middle Ages: the sixteenth and seventeenth centuries are the high noon of magic. The serious magical endeavour and the serious scientific endeavour are twins: one was sickly and died, the other strong and throve. But they were twins. They were born of the same impulse. I allow that some (certainly not all) of the early scientists were actuated by a pure love of knowledge. But if we consider the temper of that age as a whole we can discern the impulse of which I speak.

There is something which unites magic and applied science while separating both from the 'wisdom' of earlier ages. For the wise men of old the cardinal problem had been how to conform the soul to reality, and the solution had been knowledge, self-discipline, and virtue. For magic and applied science alike the problem is how to subdue reality to the wishes of men: the solution is a technique; and both, in the practice of this technique, are ready to do things hitherto regarded as disgusting and impious—such as digging up and mutilating the dead.

If we compare the chief trumpeter of the new era (Bacon) with Marlowe's Faustus, the similarity is striking. You will read in some critics that Faustus has a thirst for knowledge. In reality, he hardly mentions it. It is not truth he wants from the devils, but gold and guns and girls. 'All things that move between the quiet poles shall be at his command' and 'a sound magician is a mighty god'.[3] In the same spirit Bacon condemns those who value knowledge as an end in itself: this, for him, is to use as a mistress for pleasure what ought to be a spouse for fruit.[4] The true object is to extend Man's power to the performance of all things possible. He rejects magic because it does not work;[5] but his goal is that of the magician. In Paracelsus the characters of magician and scientist are combined. No doubt those who really founded modern science were usually those whose love of truth exceeded their love of power; in every mixed movement the efficacy comes from the good elements not from the bad. But the presence of the bad elements is not irrelevant to the direction the efficacy takes. It might be going too far to say that the modern scientific movement was tainted from its birth: but I think it would be true to say that it was born in an unhealthy neighbourhood and at an inauspicious hour. Its triumphs may have been too rapid and purchased at too high a price: reconsideration, and something like repentance, may be required.

Is it, then, possible to imagine a new Natural Philosophy, continually conscious that the 'natural object' produced by analysis and abstraction is not reality but only a view, and always correcting the abstraction? I hardly know what I am asking for. I hear rumours that Goethe's approach to nature deserves fuller consideration—that even Dr Steiner may have seen something that orthodox researchers have missed. The regenerate science which I have in mind would not do even to minerals and vegetables what modern science threatens to do to man himself. When it explained it would not explain away. When it spoke of the parts it would remember the whole. While studying the *It* it would not lose what Martin Buber calls the *Thou*-situation. The analogy between the *Tao* of Man and the instincts of an animal species would mean for it new light cast on the unknown thing, Instinct, by the inly known reality of conscience and not a reduction of conscience to the category of Instinct. Its followers would not be free with the words *only* and *merely*. In a word, it would conquer Nature without being at the same time conquered by her and buy knowledge at a lower cost than that of life.

Perhaps I am asking impossibilities. Perhaps, in the nature of things, analytical understanding must always be a basilisk which kills what it sees and only sees by killing. But if the scientists themselves cannot arrest this process before it reaches the common Reason and kills that too, then someone else must arrest it. What I most fear is the reply that I am 'only one more' obscurantist, that this barrier, like all previous barriers set up against the advance of science, can be safely passed. Such a reply springs from the fatal serialism of the modern imagination—the image of infinite unilinear progression which so haunts our minds. Because we have to use numbers so much we tend to think of every process as if it must be like the numeral series, where every step, to all eternity, is the same kind of step as the one before. I implore you to remember the Irishman and his two stoves. There are progressions in which the last step is *sui generis*—incommensurable with the others—and in which to go the whole way is to undo all the labour of your previous journey. To reduce the *Tao* to a mere natural product is a step of that kind. Up to that point, the kind of explanation which explains things away may give us something, though at a heavy cost. But you cannot go on 'explaining away' for ever: you will find that you have explained explanation itself away. You cannot go on 'seeing through' things for ever. The whole point of seeing through something is to see something through it. It is good that the window should be transparent, because the street or garden beyond it is opaque. How if you saw through the garden too? It is no use trying to 'see through' first principles. If you see through everything, then everything is transparent. But a wholly transparent world is an invisible world. To 'see through' all things is the same as not to see.

ILLUSTRATIONS OF THE *TAO*

The following illustrations of the Natural Law are col-
lected from such sources as come readily to the hand of
one who is not a professional historian. The list makes
no pretence of completeness. It will be noticed that
writers such as Locke and Hooker, who wrote within
the Christian tradition, are quoted side by side with
the New Testament. This would, of course, be absurd
if I were trying to collect independent testimonies to
the *Tao*. But (1) I am not trying to *prove* its validity by
the argument from common consent. Its validity cannot be deduced. For those who do not perceive its
rationality, even universal consent could not prove it.
(2) The idea of collecting *independent* testimonies
presupposes that 'civilizations' have arisen in the
world independently of one another; or even that
humanity has had several independent emergences on
this planet. The biology and anthropology involved in
such an assumption are extremely doubtful. It is by no

means certain that there has ever (in the sense required) been more than one civilization in all history. It is at least arguable that every civilization we find has been derived from another civilization and, in the last resort, from a single centre—'carried' like an infectious disease or like the Apostolical succession.

1. The Law of General Beneficence

(a) NEGATIVE

'I have not slain men.' (Ancient Egyptian. From the Confession of the Righteous Soul, 'Book of the Dead'. v. *Encyclopedia of Religion and Ethics* [= *ERE*], vol. v, p. 478)

'Do not murder.' (Ancient Jewish. Exodus 20:13)

'Terrify not men or God will terrify thee.' (Ancient Egyptian. Precepts of Ptahhetep. H. R. Hall, *Ancient History of the Near East*, p. 133n)

'In Nástrond (= Hell) I saw . . . murderers.' (Old Norse. *Volospá* 38, 39)

'I have not brought misery upon my fellows. I have not made the beginning of every day laborious in the sight of him who worked for me.' (Ancient Egyptian. Confession of the Righteous Soul. *ERE* v. 478)

'I have not been grasping.' (Ancient Egyptian. Ibid.)

'Who meditates oppression, his dwelling is overturned.' (Babylonian. *Hymn to Samas. ERE* v. 445)

'He who is cruel and calumnious has the character of a cat.' (Hindu. Laws of Manu. Janet, *Histoire de la Science Politique*, vol. i, p. 6)

'Slander not.' (Babylonian. *Hymn to Samas. ERE* v. 445)

'Thou shalt not bear false witness against thy neighbour.' (Ancient Jewish. Exodus 20:16)

'Utter not a word by which anyone could be wounded.' (Hindu. Janet, p. 7)

'Has he . . . driven an honest man from his family? broken up a well cemented clan?' (Babylonian. List of Sins from incantation tablets. *ERE* v. 446)

'I have not caused hunger. I have not caused weeping.' (Ancient Egyptian. *ERE* v. 478)

'Never do to others what you would not like them to do to you.' (Ancient Chinese. *Analects of Confucius*, trans. A. Waley, xv. 23; cf. xii. 2)

'Thou shalt not hate thy brother in thy heart.' (Ancient
  Jewish. Leviticus 19:17)

'He whose heart is in the smallest degree set upon goodness
  will dislike no one.' (Ancient Chinese. *Analects*, iv. 4)

(b) POSITIVE

'Nature urges that a man should wish human society to
  exist and should wish to enter it.' (Roman. Cicero, *De
  Officiis*, I. iv)

'By the fundamental Law of Nature Man [is] to be preserved as much as possible.' (Locke, *Treatises of Civil
  Govt*. ii. 3)

'When the people have multiplied, what next should be
  done for them? The Master said, Enrich them. Jan
  Ch'iu said, When one has enriched them, what next
  should be done for them? The Master said, Instruct
  them.' (Ancient Chinese. *Analects*, xiii. 9)

'Speak kindness . . . show good will.' (Babylonian. *Hymn
  to Samas. ERE* v. 445)

'Men were brought into existence for the sake of men that
  they might do one another good.' (Roman. Cicero. *De
  Off*. i. vii)

'Man is man's delight.' (Old Norse. *Hávamál* 47)

'He who is asked for alms should always give.' (Hindu. Janet, i. 7)

'What good man regards any misfortune as no concern of his?' (Roman. Juvenal xv. 140)

'I am a man: nothing human is alien to me.' (Roman. Terence, *Heaut. Tim.*)

'Love thy neighbour as thyself.' (Ancient Jewish. Leviticus 19:18)

'Love the stranger as thyself.' (Ancient Jewish. Ibid. 33, 34)

'Do to men what you wish men to do to you.' (Christian. Matthew 7:12)

2. The Law of Special Beneficence

'It is upon the trunk that a gentleman works. When that is firmly set up, the Way grows. And surely proper behaviour to parents and elder brothers is the trunk of goodness.' (Ancient Chinese. *Analects*, i. 2)

'Brothers shall fight and be each others' bane.' (Old Norse. Account of the Evil Age before the World's end, *Volospá* 45)

'Has he insulted his elder sister?' (Babylonian. List of
Sins. *ERE* v. 446)

'You will see them take care of their kindred [and] the
children of their friends . . . never reproaching them in
the least.' (Redskin. Le Jeune, quoted *ERE* v. 437)

'Love thy wife studiously. Gladden her heart all thy life
long.' (Ancient Egyptian. *ERE* v. 481)

'Nothing can ever change the claims of kinship for a right
thinking man.' (Anglo-Saxon. *Beowulf*, 2600)

'Did not Socrates love his own children, though he did so
as a free man and as one not forgetting that the gods
have the first claim on our friendship?' (Greek,
Epictetus, iii. 24)

'Natural affection is a thing right and according to
Nature.' (Greek. Ibid. 1. xi)

'I ought not to be unfeeling like a statue but should fulfil
both my natural and artificial relations, as a worshipper, a
son, a brother, a father, and a citizen.' (Greek. Ibid. iii. ii)

'This first I rede thee: be blameless to thy kindred. Take
no vengeance even though they do thee wrong.' (Old
Norse. *Sigdrifumál*, 22)

'Is it only the sons of Atreus who love their wives? For every good man, who is right-minded, loves and cherishes his own.' (Greek. Homer, *Iliad*, ix. 340)

'The union and fellowship of men will be best preserved if each receives from us the more kindness in proportion as he is more closely connected with us.' (Roman. Cicero. *De Off.* 1. xvi)

'Part of us is claimed by our country, part by our parents, part by our friends.' (Roman. Ibid. 1. vii)

'If a ruler . . . compassed the salvation of the whole state, surely you would call him Good? The Master said, It would no longer be a matter of "Good". He would without doubt be a Divine Sage.' (Ancient Chinese. *Analects*, vi. 28)

'Has it escaped you that, in the eyes of gods and good men, your native land deserves from you more honour, worship, and reverence than your mother and father and all your ancestors? That you should give a softer answer to its anger than to a father's anger? That if you cannot persuade it to alter its mind you must obey it in all quietness, whether it binds you or beats you or sends you to a war where you may get wounds or death?' (Greek. Plato, *Crito*, 51, a, b)

'If any provide not for his own, and specially for those of his own house, he hath denied the faith.' (Christian. 1 Timothy 5:8)

'Put them in mind to obey magistrates.' . . . 'I exhort that prayers be made for kings and all that are in authority.' (Christian. Titus 3:1 and 1 Timothy 2:1, 2)

3. Duties to Parents, Elders, Ancestors

'Your father is an image of the Lord of Creation, your mother an image of the Earth. For him who fails to honour them, every work of piety is in vain. This is the first duty.' (Hindu. Janet, i. 9)

'Has he despised Father and Mother?' (Babylonian. List of Sins. *ERE* v. 446)

'I was a staff by my Father's side . . . I went in and out at his command.' (Ancient Egyptian. Confession of the Righteous Soul. *ERE* v. 481)

'Honour thy Father and thy Mother.' (Ancient Jewish. Exodus 20:12)

'To care for parents.' (Greek. List of duties in Epictetus,
   iii. vii)

'Children, old men, the poor, and the sick, should be considered as the lords of the atmosphere.' (Hindu. Janet, i. 8)

'Rise up before the hoary head and honour the old man.'
   (Ancient Jewish. Leviticus 19:32)

'I tended the old man, I gave him my staff.' (Ancient
   Egyptian. *ERE* v. 481)

'You will see them take care . . . of old men.' (Redskin. Le
   Jeune, quoted *ERE* v. 437)

'I have not taken away the oblations of the blessed dead.'
   (Ancient Egyptian. Confession of the Righteous Soul.
   ERE v. 478)

'When proper respect towards the dead is shown at the
   end and continued after they are far away, the moral
   force (*tê*) of a people has reached its highest point.'
   (Ancient Chinese. *Analects*, i. 9)

4. Duties to Children and Posterity

'Children, the old, the poor, etc. should be considered as
   lords of the atmosphere.' (Hindu. Janet, i. 8)

'To marry and to beget children.' (Greek. List of duties. Epictetus, III. vii)

'Can you conceive an Epicurean commonwealth? . . . What will happen? Whence is the population to be kept up? Who will educate them? Who will be Director of Adolescents? Who will be Director of Physical Training? What will be taught?' (Greek. Ibid.)

'Nature produces a special love of offspring' and 'To live according to Nature is the supreme good.' (Roman. Cicero, *De Off*. 1. iv, and *De Legibus*, 1. xxi)

'The second of these achievements is no less glorious than the first; for while the first did good on one occasion, the second will continue to benefit the state for ever.' (Roman. Cicero. *De Off*. 1. xxii)

'Great reverence is owed to a child.' (Roman. Juvenal, xiv. 47)

'The Master said, Respect the young.' (Ancient Chinese. *Analects*, ix. 22)

'The killing of the women and more especially of the young boys and girls who are to go to make up the future strength of the people, is the saddest part . . . and

we feel it very sorely.' (Redskin. Account of the Battle
of Wounded Knee. *ERE* v. 432)

5. The Law of Justice

(a) SEXUAL JUSTICE

'Has he approached his neighbour's wife?' (Babylonian.
List of Sins. *ERE* v. 446)

'Thou shalt not commit adultery.' (Ancient Jewish.
Exodus 20:14)

'I saw in Nástrond (= Hell) . . . beguilers of others' wives.'
(Old Norse. *Volospá* 38, 39)

(b) HONESTY

'Has he drawn false boundaries?' (Babylonian. List of
Sins. *ERE* v. 446)

'To wrong, to rob, to cause to be robbed.' (Babylonian.
Ibid.)

'I have not stolen.' (Ancient Egyptian. Confession of the
Righteous Soul. *ERE* v. 478)

'Thou shalt not steal.' (Ancient Jewish. Exodus 20:15)

'Choose loss rather than shameful gains.' (Greek. Chilon
Fr. 10. Diels)

'Justice is the settled and permanent intention of rendering to each man his rights.' (Roman. Justinian, *Institutions*, 1. i)

'If the native made a "find" of any kind (e.g. a honey tree) and marked it, it was thereafter safe for him, as far as his own tribesmen were concerned, no matter how long he left it.' (Australian Aborigines. *ERE* v. 441)

'The first point of justice is that none should do any mischief to another unless he has first been attacked by the other's wrongdoing. The second is that a man should treat common property as common property, and private property as his own. There is no such thing as private property by nature, but things have become private either through prior occupation (as when men of old came into empty territory) or by conquest, or law, or agreement, or stipulation, or casting lots.' (Roman. Cicero, *De Off.* 1. vii)

(c) JUSTICE IN COURT, &c.

'Whoso takes no bribe . . . well pleasing is this to Samas.' (Babylonian. *ERE* v. 445)

'I have not traduced the slave to him who is set over him.'
(Ancient Egyptian. Confession of the Righteous Soul.
ERE v. 478)

'Thou shalt not bear false witness against thy neighbour.'
(Ancient Jewish. Exodus 20:16)

'Regard him whom thou knowest like him whom thou
knowest not.' (Ancient Egyptian. *ERE* v. 482)

'Do no unrighteousness in judgement. You must not consider the fact that one party is poor nor the fact that the
other is a great man.' (Ancient Jewish. Leviticus 19:15)

6. The Law of Good Faith and Veracity

'A sacrifice is obliterated by a lie and the merit of alms by
an act of fraud.' (Hindu. Janet, i. 6)

'Whose mouth, full of lying, avails not before thee: thou
burnest their utterance.' (Babylonian. *Hymn to Samas*.
ERE v. 445)

'With his mouth was he full of *Yea*, in his heart full of
Nay?' (Babylonian. *ERE* v. 446)

'I have not spoken falsehood.' (Ancient Egyptian.
Confession of the Righteous Soul. *ERE* v. 478)

'I sought no trickery, nor swore false oaths.' (Anglo-Saxon. *Beowulf*, 2738)

'The Master said, Be of unwavering good faith.' (Ancient Chinese. *Analects*, viii. 13)

'In Nástrond (= Hell) I saw the perjurers.' (Old Norse. *Volospá* 39)

'Hateful to me as are the gates of Hades is that man who says one thing, and hides another in his heart.' (Greek. Homer. *Iliad*, ix. 312)

'The foundation of justice is good faith.' (Roman. Cicero, *De Off.* 1. vii)

'[The gentleman] must learn to be faithful to his superiors and to keep promises.' (Ancient Chinese. *Analects*, i. 8)

'Anything is better than treachery.' (Old Norse. *Hávamál* 124)

7. The Law of Mercy

'The poor and the sick should be regarded as lords of the atmosphere.' (Hindu. Janet, i. 8)

'Whoso makes intercession for the weak, well pleasing is this to Samas.' (Babylonian. *ERE* v. 445)

'Has he failed to set a prisoner free?' (Babylonian. List of Sins. *ERE* v. 446)

'I have given bread to the hungry, water to the thirsty, clothes to the naked, a ferry boat to the boatless.' (Ancient Egyptian. *ERE* v. 446)

'One should never strike a woman; not even with a flower.' (Hindu. Janet, i. 8)

'There, Thor, you got disgrace, when you beat women.' (Old Norse. *Hárbarthsljóth* 38)

'In the Dalebura tribe a woman, a cripple from birth, was carried about by the tribes-people in turn until her death at the age of sixty-six.' . . . 'They never desert the sick.' (Australian Aborigines. *ERE* v. 443)

'You will see them take care of . . . widows, orphans, and old men, never reproaching them.' (Redskin. *ERE* v. 439)

'Nature confesses that she has given to the human race the tenderest hearts, by giving us the power to weep. This is the best part of us.' (Roman. Juvenal, xv. 131)

'They said that he had been the mildest and gentlest of the kings of the world.' (Anglo-Saxon. Praise of the hero in *Beowulf*, 3180)

'When thou cuttest down thine harvest . . . and hast forgot
a sheaf . . . thou shalt not go again to fetch it: it shall be
for the stranger, for the fatherless, and for the widow.'
(Ancient Jewish. Deuteronomy 24:19)

8. The Law of Magnanimity

(a)

'There are two kinds of injustice: the first is found in those
who do an injury, the second in those who fail to pro-
tect another from injury when they can.' (Roman.
Cicero, *De Off.* i. vii)

'Men always knew that when force and injury was offered
they might be defenders of themselves; they knew that
howsoever men may seek their own commodity, yet if
this were done with injury unto others it was not to be
suffered, but by all men and by all good means to be with-
stood.' (English. Hooker, *Laws of Eccl. Polity*, i. ix. 4)

'To take no notice of a violent attack is to strengthen the
heart of the enemy. Vigour is valiant, but cowardice is
vile.' (Ancient Egyptian. The Pharaoh Senusert III, cit.
H. R. Hall, *Ancient History of the Near East*, p. 161)

'They came to the fields of joy, the fresh turf of the
Fortunate Woods and the dwellings of the Blessed ...
here was the company of those who had suffered
wounds fighting for their fatherland.' (Roman. Virgil,
Aeneid, vi. 638–9, 660)

'Courage has got to be harder, heart the stouter, spirit
the sterner, as our strength weakens. Here lies our
lord, cut to pieces, out best man in the dust. If anyone
thinks of leaving this battle, he can howl forever.'
(Anglo-Saxon. *Maldon*, 312)

'Praise and imitate that man to whom, while life is pleasing, death is not grievous.' (Stoic. Seneca, *Ep.* liv)

'The Master said, Love learning and if attacked be ready
to die for the Good Way.' (Ancient Chinese. *Analects*,
viii. 13)

(b)

'Death is to be chosen before slavery and base deeds.'
(Roman. Cicero, *De Off.* 1, xxiii)

'Death is better for every man than life with shame.'
(Anglo-Saxon. *Beowulf*, 2890)

'Nature and Reason command that nothing uncomely, nothing effeminate, nothing lascivious be done or thought.' (Roman. Cicero, *De Off.* 1. iv)

'We must not listen to those who advise us "being men to think human thoughts, and being mortal to think mortal thoughts," but must put on immortality as much as is possible and strain every nerve to live according to that best part of us, which, being small in bulk, yet much more in its power and honour surpasses all else.' (Ancient Greek. Aristotle, *Eth. Nic.* 1177 B)

'The soul then ought to conduct the body, and the spirit of our minds the soul. This is therefore the first Law, whereby the highest power of the mind requireth obedience at the hands of all the rest.' (Hooker, op. cit. 1. viii. 6)

'Let him not desire to die, let him not desire to live, let him wait for his time . . . let him patiently bear hard words, entirely abstaining from bodily pleasures.' (Ancient Indian. Laws of Manu. *ERE* ii. 98)

'He who is unmoved, who has restrained his senses . . . is said to be devoted. As a flame in a windless place that flickers not, so is the devoted.' (Ancient Indian. *Bhagavad gita. ERE* ii 90)

(c)

'Is not the love of Wisdom a practice of death?' (Ancient Greek. Plato, *Phadeo*, 81 A)

'I know that I hung on the gallows for nine nights, wounded with the spear as a sacrifice to Odin, myself offered to Myself.' (Old Norse. *Hávamál*, 1. 10 in *Corpus Poeticum Boreale*; stanza 139 in Hildebrand's *Lieder der Älteren Edda*. 1922)

'Verily, verily I say to you unless a grain of wheat falls into the earth and dies, it remains alone, but if it dies it bears much fruit. He who loves his life loses it.' (Christian. John 12:24, 25)

NOTES

1 Men without Chests

1 *The Green Book*, pp. 19, 20.

2 Ibid., p 53.

3 *Journey to the Western Islands* (Samuel Johnson).

4 *The Prelude*, viii, ll. 549–59.

5 *The Green Book*, pp. 53–5.

6 Orbilius' book, p 5.

7 Orbilius is so far superior to Gaius and Titius that he does (pp. 19–22) contrast a piece of good writing to animals with the piece condemned. Unfortunately, however, the only superiority he really demonstrates in the second extract is its superiority in factual truth. The specifically literary problem (the use and abuse of expressions which are false *secundum litteram*) is not tackled. Orbilius indeed tells us (p. 97) that we must 'learn to distinguish between legitimate and illegitimate figurative statement', but he gives us very little help in doing so. At the same time it is

fair to record my opinion that his work is on quite a different level from *The Green Book*.

8 Ibid., p 9.

9 *Defence of Poetry*.

10 *Centuries of Meditations*, i, 12.

11 *De Civ. Dei*, xv. 22. Cf. ibid. ix. 5, xi. 28.

12 *Eth. Nic.* 1104 B.

13 Ibid. 1095 B.

14 *Laws*, 653.

15 *Republic*, 402 A.

16 A. B. Keith, s.v. 'Righteousness (Hindu)' *Enc. Religion and Ethics*, vol. x.

17 Ibid., vol. ii, p. 454 B; iv. 12 B; ix. 87 A.

18 *The Analects of Confucius*, trans. Arthur Waley, London, 1938, i. 12

19 Psalm 119:151. The word is *emeth*, 'truth'. Where the *Satya* of the Indian sources emphasizes truth as 'correspondence', *emeth* (connected with a verb that means 'to be firm') emphasizes rather the reliability or trustworthiness of truth. *Faithfulness* and *permanence* are suggested by Hebraists as alternative renderings.

Emeth is that which does not deceive, does not 'give', does not change, that which holds water. (See T. K. Cheyne in *Encyclopedia Biblica*, 1914, s.v. 'Truth'.)

20 *Republic*, 442 B, C.

21 Alanus ab Insulis. *De Planctu Naturae Prosa*, iii.

2 The Way

1 The real (perhaps unconscious) philosophy of Gaius and Titius becomes clear if we contrast the two following lists of disapprovals and approvals.

A. *Disapprovals*: A mother's appeal to a child to be 'brave' is 'nonsense' (*Green Book*, p. 62). The reference of the word 'gentleman' is 'extremely vague' (ibid.) 'To call a man a coward tells us really nothing about what he does' (p. 64). Feelings about a country or empire are feelings 'about nothing in particular' (p. 77).

B. *Approvals*: Those who prefer the arts of peace to the arts of war (it is not said in what circumstances) are such that 'we may want to call them wise men' (p. 65). The pupil is expected 'to believe in a democractic community life' (p. 67). 'Contact with the ideas of other people is, as we know, healthy' (p. 86). The reason for bathrooms ('that people are healthier and pleasanter to meet when they are clean') is 'too obvious to need mentioning' (p. 142). It will be seen that comfort and security, as known to a suburban street in peace-time, are the ultimate values: those things which can alone produce or spiritualize comfort and security are mocked. Man lives by bread alone, and the ultimate source of bread is the baker's van: peace matters more than honour and can be preserved by jeering at colonels and reading newspapers.

2 The most determined effort which I know to construct a theory of value on the basis of 'satisfaction of impulses' is that of Dr I. A. Richards (*Principles of Literary Criticism*, 1924). The old objection to defining Value as Satisfaction is the universal value judgement that 'it is better to be Socrates dissatisfied than a pig satisfied'. To meet

this Dr Richards endeavours to show that our impulses can be arranged in a hierarchy and some satisfactions preferred to others without an appeal to any criterion other than satisfaction. He does this by the doctrine that some impulses are more 'important' than others—an *important* impulse being one whose frustration involves the frustration of other impulses. A good systematization (i.e. the good life) consists in satisfying as many impulses as possible; which entails satisfying the 'important' at the expense of the 'unimportant'. The objections to this scheme seem to me to be two:

(1) Without a theory of immortality it leaves no room for the value of noble death. It may, of course, be said that a man who has saved his life by treachery will suffer for the rest of that life from frustration. But not, surely, frustration of *all* his impulses? Whereas the dead man will have *no* satisfaction. Or is it maintained that since he had no unsatisfied impulses he is better off than the disgraced

and living man? This at once raises the second objection.

(2) Is the value of a systematization to be judged by the presence of satisfactions or the absence of dissatisfactions? The extreme case is that of the dead man in whom satisfactions and dissatisfactions (on the modern view) both equal zero, as against the successful traitor who can still eat, drink, sleep, scratch and copulate, even if he cannot have friend-ship or love or self-respect. But it arises at other levels. Suppose *A* has only 500 impulses and all are satisfied, and that *B* has 1200 impulses whereof 700 are satisfied and 500 not: which has the better systematiza-tion? There is no doubt which Dr Richards actually prefers—he even praises art on the ground that it makes us 'discontented' with ordinary crudities! (op. cit., p. 230). The only trace I find of a philosophical basis for this preference is the statement that 'the more complex an activity the more conscious it is'

(p. 109). But if satisfaction is the only value, why should increase of consciousness be good? For consciousness is the condition of all dissastisfactions as well as of all satisfactions. Dr Richards's system gives no support to his (and our) actual preference for civil life over savage and human over animal—or even for life over death.

3 The desperate expedients to which a man can be driven if he attempts to base value on fact are well illustrated by Dr C. H. Waddington's fate in *Science and Ethics*. Dr Waddington here explains that 'existence is its own justification' (p. 14), and writes: 'An existence which is essentially evolutionary is itself the justification for an evolution towards a more comprehensive existence' (p. 17). I do not think Dr Waddington is himself at ease in this view, for he does endeavour to recommend the course of evolution to us on three grounds other than its mere occurrence. (*a*) That the later stages include or 'comprehend' the earlier. (*b*) That T. H. Huxley's picture of Evolution

will not revolt you if you regard it from an 'actu-arial' point of view. (*c*) That, any way, after all, it isn't half so bad as people make out ('not so morally offensive that we cannot accept it', p. 18). These three palliatives are more creditable to Dr Waddington's heart than his head and seem to me to give up the main position. If Evolution is praised (or, at least, apologized for) on the ground of *any* properties it exhibits, then we are using an external standard and the attempt to make existence its own justification has been abandoned. If that attempt is maintained, why does Dr Waddington concentrate on Evolution: i.e. on a temporary phase of organic existence in one planet? This is 'geocentric'. If Good = 'what-ever Nature happens to be doing', then surely we should notice what Nature is doing as a whole; and Nature as a whole, I understand, is working steadily and irreversibly towards the final extinc-tion of all life in every part of the universe, so that Dr Waddington's ethics, stripped of their unaccountable bias towards such a parochial affair as tellurian biology, would leave murder and suicide our only duties. Even this, I confess, seems to me a lesser objection than the discrepancy between Dr Waddington's first principle and the value judgements men actually make. To value anything simply because it occurs is in fact to worship success, like Quislings or men of Vichy. Other philosophies more wicked have been devised: none more vulgar. I am far from suggesting that Dr Waddington practises in real life such grovelling prostration before the *fait accompli*. Let us hope that *Rasselas*, chap. 22, gives the right picture of what his philosophy amounts to in action. ('The philosopher, supposing the rest vanquished, rose up and departed with the air of a man that had co-operated with the present system.')

4 See Appendix.

5 *Analects of Confucius*, xv. 39.

6 *Eth. Nic.* 1095 B, 1140 B, 1151 A.

7 John 7:49. The speaker said it in malice, but with more truth than he meant. Cf. John 13:51.

8 Mark 16:6.

9 *Republic,* 402 A

10 Philippians 3:6.

3 The Abolition of Man

1 *The Boke Named the Governour,* 1. iv: 'Al men except physitions only shulde be excluded and kepte out of the norisery.' 1 vi: 'After that a childe is come to seuen yeres of age . . . the most sure counsaile is to withdrawe him from all company of women.'

2 *Some Thoughts concerning Education,* §7: 'I will also advise his *Feet to be wash'd* every Day in cold Water, and to have his Shoes so thin that they might leak and *let in Water,* whenever he comes near it.' § 174: 'If he have a poetick vein, 'tis to me the strangest thing in the World that the Father should desire or suffer it to be cherished or improved. Methinks the Parents should labour to have it stifled and suppressed as much as may be.' Yet Locke is one of our most sensible writers on education.

3 *Dr Faustus*, 77–90.

4 *Advancement of Learning*, Bk 1 (p. 60 in Ellis and Spedding, 1905; p. 35 in Everyman Edition).

5 *Filum Labyrinthi*, i.